MW01616568

Translated by Rose Brichard

The Pearl

BY JOHN STEINBECK

Bright
≡Summaries.com

JOHN STEINBECK

AMERICAN WRITER

- **Born in Salinas, California in 1902**
- **Died in New York in 1968**
- **Notable works:**
  - *Of Mice and Men* (1937), novel
  - *The Grapes of Wrath* (1939), novel
  - *East of Eden* (1952), novel

John Steinbeck (1902-1968) is an American writer whose works (including *Of Mice and Men*, 1937; *The Grapes of Wrath*, 1939; *East of Eden*, 1952) are drawn together by their setting in the author's home-state of California and their themes of hardship among rural populations. Steinbeck worked as a reporter for the International Herald Tribune during the Second World War, and was awarded the Nobel Prize for literature in 1962. Many film adaptations of his work exist which have also contributed to his fame and popularity.

THE PEARL

A POISONED CHALICE

- **Genre:** novel
- **Reference edition:** Steinbeck, J. (no date) The Pearl. [online]. PTbeach. [Accessed 18 July 2016]. Available from: <http://www.ptbeach.com/cms/lib02/NJ01000839/Centricity/Domain/211/The-Pearl-John-Steinbeck.pdf>
- **First edition:** 1947
- **Themes:** evil, temptation, racism, greed

The Pearl was first published in 1947 and tells the story of a poor Mexican fisherman named Kino who discovers an enormous valuable pearl which he hopes will bring him and his family prosperity and education. This parable-like novel explores the adventures and tragedies of Kino and his family in the wake of his discovery of the pearl. *The Pearl* exposes social injustices and the hardship suffered by indigenous people in colonised territories, a theme which recurs throughout Steinbeck's oeuvre.

Before publishing this work, Steinbeck had already touched upon the idea of discovering an enormous pearl in his *Sea of Cortez* texts, which he wrote during a scientific expedition in the Gulf of California in 1940.

SUMMARY

A poor Native American fishing family sees its life irreversibly altered when a colossal and valuable pearl falls into its possession.

Kino, a young and healthy man lives with his reticent but determined wife Juana and their baby boy Coyotito in a Native American village in Mexico. One day, Coyotito is stung by a deadly scorpion; already, happy family life has been disrupted. Juana tries to save her son from the poison by sucking it from his wound and tells Kino to call the doctor. However, Kino is convinced that the doctor won't take the time and trouble to come to a Native American village, so Juana decides that they will go to La Paz and see the doctor themselves. When they arrive, the doctor pretends to be out and refuses to help little Coyotito, as his parents are poor.

THE PEARL

Having left the town of La Paz, Kino and Juana go fishing for pearls on his grandfather's canoe - the only thing of any worth they own and their means of survival - just as they do every day. Before getting on the boat, Juana dresses Coyotito's wound with brown algae, said to be a remedy for children's ailments. When they are fishing, Kino finds an incredible pearl; lucid and huge in size.

Rumours about Kino's discovery quickly spread through the village and the town. Surrounded by the other villagers in his hut, Kino talks of all the wonderful things the pearl will secure for him - a church wedding, new clothes, a gun and, above all, he will be able to send Coyotito to school to help him break the cycle of white intellectual supremacy. Little by little, desire and greed emerge among the white townspeople; Kino is now an enemy. This is the beginning of a seemingly never-ending quest to steal the pearl from Kino, which will involve trickery, as is the case with the corrupt sellers, and violence, as demonstrated when Kino is mysteriously attacked.

GREED

At nightfall that same day, the town priest comes to see Kino to congratulate him and warn him not to forget the Church. Next, the doctor arrives. He tricks Kino and Juana into thinking that little Coyotito is still in danger, and gives him medicine which leaves the child in agony.

An hour later, the doctor returns to "save" the baby's life. Once Coyotito is well again, the doctor asks Kino to cough up the medical fee. He tells him he will pay the bill the following day once he has sold the pearl. The doctor pretends that this is the first he has heard of this pearl, and offers to take it for safekeeping. Kino turns him down, but can't help his eyes wandering towards the place where he has hidden his treasure. During the night, someone tries to steal the pearl, but Kino attacks them with his knife. The thief fights back and escapes before Kino can see who it is. Already, Juana wants to get rid of the pearl; she thinks it can only bring them bad luck, while Kino still sees it as the gateway to all their dreams.

SELLING THE PEARL

The next day, Kino and Juana go to the pearl-sellers auction, followed by a crowd of villagers and townspeople. Kino does not know that the market is actually a sham; all the white pearl-sellers pretend to be independent to create false competition and get the price as low as possible when in fact they all answer to one person. The first merchant Kino goes to tells him the pearl is worthless since its size means no-one except perhaps a museum would have any use for it. Kino doesn't believe him, so the merchant calls on the other buyers who are, of course, all in on the scam; they back up his valuation. Kino is furious and declares that he will go and sell it himself in the capital to escape the pearl merchants' trap.

At nightfall, Kino is attacked once again. He is injured, but the pearl remains intact and in his possession. Juana is terrified and asks Kino once again to throw the cursed pearl back into the ocean. He refuses, telling her it is his decision because he is the man. He announces that the following day he intends to go to the capital in the canoe. Juana pretends to agree to this, but secretly tries to get rid of the pearl during the night, feeling that it will only bring evil towards them.

Kino hears Juana during the night and follows her. He realises what she is doing and beats her to stop her from throwing it away. Someone emerges from the dark and attacks Kino. Kino fights back and accidentally kills the stranger. He hides his body in the bushes and tells Juana to go and get

Coyotito and some belongings so they can leave straight away. He goes to the boat and discovers that someone has destroyed it. He is enraged and runs back to the hut to tell Juana, where he finds his home on fire. Juana is terrified, so they take Coyotito and go to hide out in Kino's brother, Juan Tômas', hut. Juan tells the other villagers that Kino and his family died in the blaze. Kino tells his brother that they are going to flee.

THE ESCAPE

Kino and his family leave as soon as possible. They only travel under the cover of night and always erase their tracks. One day, Kino catches sight of two trackers and a man with a gun, though they have not yet seen them. Kino and Juana panic, and flee to the mountains to hide out in a cave. The trackers follow them and camp out beneath the cave for the night. Kino decides to sneak down and attack the gunman and steal his weapon. Coyotito stays with Juana and begins crying. The gunman thinks that it's an animal and shoots towards the noise; little Coyotito is killed. Kino attacks him and the other two men, killing them. When he returns, he finds out that Coyotito is dead. He and his wife return to the village side by side, and Kino finally follows Juana's advice and throws the pearl into the sea.

CHARACTER STUDY

KINO

Kino is a man from an indigenous Mexican village. Like the other villagers, he just about makes ends meet through pearl-hunting. He is young, fit, determined, and proud of his ancestry and local customs (most importantly embodied by his grandfather's canoe). Nevertheless, this pride and determination diminishes when he is around white people; he feels inferior. The desire to be more like the white people also makes it difficult for Kino to write new songs, something typical in his culture. Now he is left with only the songs of his ancestors, moving further and further away from his roots.

As the novel progresses, Kino's character undergoes a transformation. At the beginning, he has an ardent desire to have what the white people have, such as a gun and access to education; he does not want to be Native American anymore. As the curse brings various misfortunes upon him, he moves closer towards an animalistic nature. In the mountains, he sniffs the earth and hides in the bushes like an animal being hunted. He again loses his humanity when he massacres the three men; the promise of wealth and prosperity has led Kino to be totally transformed.

JUANA

Juana is Kino's wife. She takes care of and upholds their little family and their household, and is presented as loving and intuitive. She shows a great strength of mind and character when she finds herself in emergencies and difficult situations, such as caring for her injured baby or trying to throw the pearl into the sea.

As a woman, Juana is subjected to her husband's will. She walks behind him when they flee and never tries to take the lead. Even when Kino hurts her, she does not retaliate, accepting her fate at the hands of her husband. However, as the plot moves on, Juana begins to rebel and moves towards an equal footing with Kino. When they go back to the village after their son's death, she and Kino walk side by side. She shows herself to be brave and perseverant when the family flees, and remains dignified in the face of tragedy.

While it might appear that Juana often lives in her husband's shadow, she is always several steps ahead of him mentally. Right from the start, she knows that the pearl will bring them bad luck. She is also the first to react when Coyotito is stung by the scorpion.

THE NATIVE AMERICAN VILLAGERS

The villagers are part of the same tribe as Kino. They are present at all important community events, and it is for this reason that they come with Kino and his family when they go to see the doctor and to the pearl auction

They represent indigenous customs and traditions. Just like the protagonist, they are ashamed of their roots. For example, though the receptionist in the doctor's office is herself a Native American, she refuses to speak to Kino in her native tongue. They too wish for wealth and education, but unlike the townspeople, they do not try to steal the pearl; they are happy for Kino.

The difference between Kino and the rest of the villagers is the fact that Kino wants to escape his social standing and break the barriers put in place by the white townspeople. The Native Americans think that he should just be happy with the low price that the pearl merchants offer him.

THE WHITE TOWNSPEOPLE

The nearby town of La Paz is populated by white people, who see the Native Americans as inferior. The doctor treats them like animals, saying that he is a doctor and not a vet. These townspeople are consumed with greed, and are happy to use Kino's lack of education against him in their attempts to steal the pearl. They are never satisfied with what they have; even though the doctor is already rich and lives in relative opulence, he dreams of going back to Paris.

ANALYSIS

THE THEME OF MUSIC AND SONG

Singing is something which punctuates the novel, giving it its own rhythm and acting as a representation of Kino's emotions. Although Steinbeck never tells the reader any actual lyrics, singing is something which is entirely embedded in the narrative and almost becomes a character in its own right, as shown here: "a savage, secret, dangerous melody, and underneath, the Song of the Family cried plaintively." (p. 3).

Singing is inextricably linked to the protagonist's culture. Trying to be more like the white townspeople, Kino distances himself from indigenous traditions and culture and finds himself unable to write new songs.

The types of song featured in *The Pearl* are:

- Songs of happiness: the sound of safety and family which Juana hums while making breakfast;
- Songs of evil: representing the scorpion's sting, the townspeople's greed and trickery, and the attempts to steal the pearl;
- Songs about the Pearl: initially, this is a song about Kino, as he sees his hopes and dreams reflected in this incredible pearl. However, the pearl's sheen begins to fade and Kino cannot see the curse it represents.

COLONISATION

Kino's story takes place against a backdrop of the white colonisation of Mexico. It is worth bearing in mind the historical facts. In 1519, the Spaniard Hernan Cortes (Spanish conqueror, 1485-1547), landed in Mexico with armed troops; this was the beginning of the end for the Aztec empire. In the 16th and 17th centuries, Spain gradually colonised all of Central America, stripping it of its riches and forcing new rulers into power. Through violence and massacres, they imposed Christianity and their customs on the indigenous populations, which they considered to be an inferior race.

In the novel, Steinbeck offers a critique of colonisation, showing how white townspeople exploit the indigenous communities:

- Chapters 4-5: the doctor tricks Kino into believing that his son's life is still in danger and pretends to save his life, with the sole goal of extracting money from him.
- Chapter 4: the priest comes to remind Kino how important it is to be charitable towards the church. He tells Kino that a story just like his can be found "in the books", about a man who brought peace to all of Mexico, urging him to be generous in the same way.
- Chapter 6: the pearl merchants work together to exploit Kino. Kino is sure that the pearl is valuable and refuses to believe the white buyers.

In spite of themselves and perhaps without truly realising it, the Native Americans begin to mimic European customs and habits in their hopes to achieve a similar standard of living as the white townspeople:

- Chapter 1: when Coyotito is bitten by the scorpion, Juana recites an old prayer of the indigenous community mixed with the Ave Maria, borrowed from Christianity;
- Chapter 3: Juana makes a wish that an enormous pearl is hidden within the oyster Kino catches. She nonetheless notes that you must remain humble towards "God and the gods", thus referring to both a Christian God and her own beliefs;
- Chapter 4: Kino hopes that the pearl will be the gateway to all his dreams of having a similar standard of living as the white people; having a gun, seeing his son receive an education, getting married, having shoes, etc.

Steinbeck uses *The Pearl* to denounce the injustice of colonisation, something he himself found intolerable and barbaric. The author argues that the indigenous people should be proud of their customs and stay loyal to tradition. Analysing the situation through this lens is perhaps linked to Steinbeck's own experience in life. He draws a parallel between his childhood in the countryside and the Native Americans. When he was growing up, his forays into the town led him to hate the townspeople and their attempts to exploit the rural populations.

BINARY OPPOSITIONS: GOOD VS EVIL AND INDIGENOUS VS WHITE

In the novel, Steinbeck creates an explicit binary opposition between the indigenous people and the white townspeople. Through their actions, clothes and attitudes, these two groups are aligned with good and evil respectively:

- Food: the Native Americans eat healthily – corn cakes and beans, while the white people stuff themselves with sweet biscuits and chocolates. Some of them, like the doctor, are obese;
- Clothes: the villagers wear simple and practical clothes with dignity. When Kino and Juana go to sell the pearl, they put on their best clothes - though they still well-worn - and wear them with pride. On the other hand, the white buyers dress in grotesque luxury, but seem to be almost in disguise (like the doctor);
- Housing: the villagers live in simple huts which have no doors, filled with natural light. The townspeople live in brick houses, blocking out the world with doors and locks. For example, Kino has to go to knock on the doctor's door; it is quickly slammed in his face;
- Speech and dialogue: the villagers speak plainly and honestly. They are easily influenced and not suspicious of others, whereas the townspeople continually say things they don't mean to get what they want, and use this to trick Kino and his family. They use their access to education to exploit those who are not so lucky.

FURTHER REFLECTION

SOME QUESTIONS TO THINK ABOUT...

- Find examples of imagery and word choice used by the author to show how the town itself is "like a colonial animal".
- Is the author's passion for biology evident in the text? Justify your answer with several examples from the novel.
- How does the doctor's house reflect his personality?
- Look at the vocabulary used to express fear in the first three chapters. Does it reflect the plot development? Justify your answer.
- In your opinion, what does Kino's black dog represent?
- In your opinion, why does Juana insist that Kino throws the pearl in the sea himself at the end of the novel?
- Look at chapters 9 and 10. Show how the author illustrates Kino becoming more and more like an animal.
- What is Steinbeck's opinion on colonisation and colonialism? What factors in his own life might have influenced this?
- Which other Steinbeck novels can be considered as strong social critiques?
- Find some other novels which explore the history of colonisation. Compare and contrast with *The Pearl*.

We want to hear from you!
Leave a comment on your online library
and share your favourite books on social media!

FURTHER READING

REFERENCE EDITION

- Steinbeck, J. (no date) *The Pearl*. [online]. PTbeach. [Accessed 18 July 2016]. Available from: <http://www.ptbeach.com/cms/lib02/NJ01000839/Centricity/Domain/211/The-Pearl-John-Steinbeck.pdf>

FILM ADAPTATION

- *The Pearl*. (1947) [Film]. Emilio Fernandez. Dir. Mexico: Film Asociados Mexico-Americanos.

MORE FROM BRIGHTSUMMARIES.COM

- Reading guide - *Of Mice and Men* by John Steinbeck
- Reading Guide - *The Grapes of Wrath* by John Steinbeck

www.brightsummaries.com

Ebook EAN: 9782806280374

Paperback EAN: 9782806282965

Legal Deposit: D/2016/12603/295

Cover: © Primento

Digital conception by Primento, the digital partner of publishers.

Made in the USA
Monee, IL
10 June 2024